# THE DAILY SPARK

*180 easy-to-use lessons and class activities!*

# THE DAILY SPARK

Critical Thinking
Journal Writing
Poetry
Pre-Algebra
SAT: English Test Prep
Shakespeare
Spelling & Grammar
U.S. History
Vocabulary
Writing

THE

# *DAILY SPARK*

# ***Poetry***

This edition published by Spark Publishing.

Spark Publishing
A Division of SparkNotes LLC
120 Fifth Avenue, 8th Floor
New York, NY 10011

ISBN 1-4114-0222-7

Please submit changes or report errors to *www.sparknotes.com/errors*.

Printed and bound in the United States.

Written by Lise Clavel.

*A Barnes & Noble Publication*

# Introduction

The *Daily Spark* series gives teachers an easy way to transform downtime into productive time. The 180 exercises—one for each day of the school year—will take students five to ten minutes to complete and can be used at the beginning of class, in the few moments before turning to a new subject, or at the end of class.

The exercises in this book may be photocopied and handed out to the class, projected as a transparency, or even read aloud. In addition to class time use, they can be assigned as homework exercises or extra credit problems.

The *Poetry Daily Spark* gets students excited about poetry by quoting colorful modern poems, explaining basic concepts like metaphor and meter, and showing students how to write poems of their own. Students who think of poetry as esoteric or boring will change their minds after encountering prose poems, composing funny haikus, and writing melodramatic verse about their own lives.

Spark your students' interest with the *Poetry Daily Spark*!

# What Is a Poem?

What's your definition of a poem? Think about all the different kinds of poems you've read throughout your life, both in school and out.

Jot down a few elements that, in your opinion, most poems share.

# The Mind's Palm Tree

In his poem "Of Mere Being," Wallace Stevens imagines a palm tree that stands at the end of the mind, "beyond the last thought." This tree symbolizes Stevens's idea of heaven. What is the "beyond" that you imagine?

Using short, declarative sentences like Stevens's, write a poem that describes your own beyond, your own heaven.

# Walking on the Moon

How would it feel to move around in a gravity-free world? What would it be like to see the Earth from such a distance?

Write a poem about walking on the Moon.

# Poetry's Speakers

In poetry, we talk about the person narrating the poem as the **speaker**. This is because the speaker of that particular poem often does not hold the same point of view as the poet. When you yourself write poetry, the same rules apply—you don't always have to be the speaker. You can write from many different points of view.

To experiment with this idea, write a very short poem about something that happened today. Then write the poem again from a different, perhaps opposing, perspective.

# "Pied Beauty"

*Glory be to God for dappled things—*
*For skies of couple-colour as a brinded cow;*
*For rose-moles all in stipple upon trout that swim;*
*Fresh-firecoal chestnut-falls; finches' wings;*
*Landscape plotted and pieced—fold, fallow,*
*and plough;*
*And áll trádes, their gear and tackle and trim.*
*All things counter, original, spare, strange;*
*Whatever is fickle, freckled (who knows how?)*
*With swift, slow; sweet, sour; adazzle, dim;*
*He fathers-forth whose beauty is past change:*
*Praise him.*

Gerard Manley Hopkins invented the **curtal sonnet**, of which "Pied Beauty" is an example. The curtal sonnet, as opposed to the Shakespearean and Petrarchan sonnets, has only ten full lines, rather than the other versions' fourteen. The last line of a curtal sonnet consists of only two stressed syllables ("praise him," in "Pied Beauty"). This kind of double stress is called a **spondee**.

Write a ten-line poem that ends with a two-word line.

# To Make a Bed

Think of the format of a food recipe: first there is the list of ingredients you will need, then the explanation of how to mix the ingredients together, and finally the cooking time.

Using this format, write a recipe poem that has nothing to do with food. You might write a recipe for how to make good conversation, how to climb a tree, how to ski, or how to fall in love.

# No First or Last

In an untitled poem, Mina Loy makes many sweeping statements, such as "There is no First or Last / Only equality." Do you agree with this statement?

Write a poem in which you either defend or contradict this statement.

# Mother, Father

Write a poem in which you describe one of your parents. Try not to describe this parent's character directly. Instead, make the poem hinge around just one memory that sums up your mother's or father's personality.

# Ghosts, Monsters, Bullies

What did you fear when you were a child? Thunderstorms, spiders, your parents divorcing?

Write a poem about one of your childhood fears.

# The Art of Losing

The poem form called the **villanelle** involves lots of repetition. In Elizabeth Bishop's villanelle "One Art," the line "The art of losing isn't hard to master" is repeated several times.

Try writing a version of the villanelle by using the same line to begin and end your poem.

# Life and Milk

Billy Collins's poem "The Lanyard" is touching and sad at the same time. In it, Collins describes giving a lanyard (a braided plastic necklace) to his mother:

*She gave me life and milk from her breasts,*
*and I gave her a lanyard.*

Collins suggests that a lanyard is totally insufficient thanks for his mother, the woman who did everything for him. At the same time, he is amused by the memory of his younger self, who meant well.

Think of a gift you made for one of your parents or for a friend when you were a child, and write a poem about it.

# Sonnet 130

*My mistress' eyes are nothing like the sun;*
*Coral is far more red than her lips' red;*
*If snow be white, why then her breasts are dun;*
*If hairs be wires, black wires grow on her head.*
*I have seen roses damasked, red and white,*
*But no such roses see I in her cheeks,*
*And in some perfumes is there more delight*
*Than in the breath that from my mistress reeks.*
*I love to hear her speak, yet well I know,*
*That music hath a far more pleasing sound.*
*I grant I never saw a goddess go;*
*My mistress when she walks treads on the ground.*
*And yet, by heaven, I think my love as rare*
*As any she belied with false compare.*

In Sonnet 130, William Shakespeare writes about a lover, who is not beautiful in a traditional sense. But despite this, the speaker loves her: "And yet, by heaven, I think my love as rare / As any she belied with false compare."

Write a poem about someone who is not considered attractive (feel free to interpret "attractive" in any way you like), but who you think is amazing nonetheless.

# I'd Never Have Wakened

*Did he appear*
*because I fell asleep*
*thinking of him?*
*If only I'd known I was dreaming,*
*I'd never have wakened.*

In this poem by Ono No Komachi, the speaker imagines staying in her dream instead of returning to her regular waking life. Have you ever had a dream that you didn't want to wake up from?

Imagine the continuation of that dream—the part you didn't get to experience because you woke up—and write a poem about it.

# Zeugma

In the third line of his poem "What the Gypsies Told My Grandmother While She Was Still a Young Girl," Charles Simic uses a **zeugma:**

*You'll chop onions and pieces of your heart into the same hot skillet.*

A zeugma is a device in which one word applies to two nouns in different ways. In Simic's poem, "chop" describes an everyday activity and acts as a painful metaphor. Another example of a zeugma is "He stole my money and my soul."

Come up with a zeugma of your own and use it in a poem.

# Stuck

Have you ever been locked in a closet or stuck in an elevator? What did you feel like doing? What did you think about? Is there one thing you really wished you had with you, like a chocolate bar or a CD player? Don't feel that you have to answer all of these questions; just use them for inspiration.

Whether you're drawing on personal experience or relying on your imagination, write a poem about the feeling of being confined to a small place for an indefinite amount of time.

# “Archaic Torso of Apollo”

*We cannot know his legendary head*
*with eyes like ripening fruit. And yet his torso*
*is still suffused with brilliance from inside,*
*like a lamp, in which his gaze, now turned to low,*

*gleams in all its power. Otherwise*
*the curved breast could not dazzle you so, nor could*
*a smile run through the placid hips and thighs*
*to that dark center where procreation flared.*

*Otherwise this stone would seem defaced*
*beneath the translucent cascade of the shoulders*
*and would not glisten like a wild beast’s fur:*

*would not, from all the borders of itself,*
*burst like a star: for here there is no place*
*that does not see you. You must change your life.*

In this poem by Rainer Maria Rilke, the speaker describes seeing a statue that has a powerful effect on him. The poem ends with the line “You must change your life.” Have you ever had a sudden realization after observing an object or an event? Describe the object or event in your poem and then end with a line as dramatic as Rilke’s last line.

# Around the Block

Imagine you're walking down a block in your neighborhood. Write a poem in which you describe everything you see along the way, from puddles to pieces of trash, from lost gloves to chipped paint on the curb.

# Singing Along

Think of a song you've been listening to a lot recently. Then write a poem or a song inspired by that song's lyrics.

# Dear Kiddo

Write a poem in the form of a letter to your future child. What do you want him or her to know about you? What kind of person do you hope this child will turn out to be? What do you want him or her to know about the world he or she is about to enter? Don't feel that you have to answer all of these questions; just use them as inspiration.

# "In a Station of the Metro"

*The apparition of these faces in the crowd;*
*Petals on a wet, black bough.*

This poem by Ezra Pound offers a single, clear image. Think of just one image you'd like to express. Then try to distill everything you'd like to say about this image into a two-line poem.

# Chewing the Scenery

Think of the best scene from one of your favorite movies. Write a poem from the perspective of one of the characters in that scene.

# Recent Disaster

In "Musée des Beaux Arts," by W. H. Auden, the speaker muses about a painting that depicts Icarus falling from the sky into the sea. Even while this disaster happens, notes the speaker of the poem, ordinary life continues:

*. . . the ploughman may*
*Have heard the splash, the forsaken cry,*
*But for him it was not an important failure . . .*

In a poem, describe a recent disaster and the everyday life that carried on as the disaster was happening.

# Beloved Toy

Think of an object—perhaps something from your childhood—that you love even though you don't use it now.

Write a poem with two stanzas. In the first stanza, describe the object and what you used to do with it. In the second stanza, describe a moment from your childhood in which you felt strongly about the object.

# Ten Lovely Words

Write a list of ten of your favorite words. Include words you like because of their meaning and words you like because of their sound. Then use all of these words in a poem.

# My Victorian Nightgown

Pick any poem you like (a medium-length poem would be best), and copy it out, leaving plenty of space between each line. Then make a new poem by adding a line of your own between each pair of original lines.

For example, if you were to choose Sylvia Plath's poem "Morning Song," you might write something like this (the added line is bold):

*One cry, and I stumble from bed, cow-heavy and floral*
***Bewildered with sleep***
*In my Victorian nightgown.*

You can play around with the other poet's punctuation and even with verb tenses or noun articles.

# Counting Song Syllables

Write down a few lines from one of your favorite songs. Make these the first few lines of a poem.

Try to write several new lines, each of which has the same number of syllables as the lines of the song lyrics. Counting syllables is a great way to discipline yourself in your writing, and it can even help you condense your language.

# Battered Down Doors

In "Women," Alice Walker pays tribute to her mother's generation, which "battered down / doors" and fought for future generations.

Write a tribute to a group of people who have accomplished something you respect. As you write, experiment with the effect a one- or two-word line can have on the reader.

# Free from Grammar

Poetry often tries to capture an event or an emotion in a way that "regular" writing cannot. Because conventional rules of grammar don't apply in poetry, writing poetry can give you a feeling of freedom.

Write a paragraph about what happened to you last night, and then turn that paragraph into a poem. Which form do you prefer, paragraph or poem? Why?

# “We Real Cool”

Gwendolyn Brooks has said that the speakers of her poem “We Real Cool” are high school–age delinquents skulking in a pool hall (“We real cool. We / Left school”), uncertain about their identities and their future (“We / Die soon”), but still able to “talk the talk.”

Write a poem spoken from the perspective of your group of friends.

# Love Is Like . . .

Consider the phrase "love is like . . . ." Think about what love is like to you, and write a poem comparing love to an object, experience, food—anything you want.

# Three Silent Things

*These be*
*Three silent things:*
*The falling snow . . . the hour*
*Before the dawn . . . the mouth of one*
*Just dead.*

This untitled five-line poem is a **cinquain**. Cinquains consist of one five-line stanza (just like a quatrain is one four-line stanza). Note that Adelaide Crapsey's poem has a special style in addition to its cinquain form: the first and last lines are two syllables each; the second line has four syllables, the third has six, and the fourth has eight.

Write a cinquain about anything you want.

# Your Chosen Poet

Read several poems by any poet you choose. Try to get a feel for that poet's style and voice; observe what he or she does with meter, rhyme, and word choice. Pick a topic, then write a poem that emulates your chosen poet's style.

# My Friend in Nature

"My Friend Tree," by Lorine Niedecker, uses simple language:

*My friend tree*
*I sawed you down . . .*

Write a poem in which you address an object in nature. Make your poem a **narrative** (or story) told in very simple words, just as Niedecker does. Try not to use punctuation.

# Like Paper

Write a poem that focuses on the movement of one object or animal, or even a person.

Try not to use a lot of *-ly* adverbs (such as *quickly, sweetly,* or *angrily*). Instead, use similes that will get your point across. For example, you might write, "The branches moved like paper floating under water," instead of "the branches swayed softly back and forth."

# A Hard Question

In "Making a Fist" by Naomi Shihab Nye, the speaker asks her mother how you know if you're going to die. The mother answers, "'When you can no longer make a fist.'" Think of a hard question you asked an adult when you were young. How did he or she answer?

Try capturing your question and the adult's answer in a poem.

# Trying Again

Think of a time you tried to explain something but just couldn't put it into words. Maybe you were trying to tell someone how you felt about him or her; maybe you were in the midst of a fight and couldn't express yourself.

Try to put your feelings into words, this time in a poem.

# I Hate My Job

In his poem "Hay for the Horses," Gary Snyder writes of a sixty-eight-year-old man who has worked hauling hay all his life. The man says, "'I thought, that day I started, / I sure would hate to do this all my life.'" But the man has done just what he didn't want to do—stuck with a job he dislikes.

Think of a job or chore that you have been doing or have done that you can't imagine doing as an adult. Imagine that you have had to keep doing this job for fifty-seven years, and write a poem about it from the perspective of your adult self.

# Alphabet Ode

Pick one letter of the alphabet and write a poem in which the first word of each line begins with that letter.

If you're really daring, try making the last word of every line start with the same letter too.

# Unusual Emotion

Write down one emotion that you want to convey in a poem. List a few of the obvious experiences that could make you feel that emotion—and then ignore the list.

In your poem, describe an event you wouldn't normally associate with the emotion you've chosen.

# Does the World Need Words?

In the poem "Words," Dana Gioia writes,

*The world does not need words. It articulates itself*
*in sunlight, leaves, and shadows.*

Think of other things that don't speak, and write a poem about how these things express themselves. How does an apple, or a spoon, or a house communicate?

# The Hottest Blood of All

An excerpt from "Whales Weep Not!" by D. H. Lawrence:

*They say the sea is cold, but the sea contains*
*the hottest blood of all, and the wildest, the most urgent.*

Lawrence begins "Whales Weep Not!" by repeating a conventional idea about something in nature: "They say the sea is cold." He goes on to contradict this idea and describe the sea in his own way.

Pick something you think is often seen or described incorrectly, and then write a poem about that thing from your own perspective. If you want, you can start the poem with the phrase "They say," the way Lawrence does.

# An Everyday Pair

David Lehman wrote a poem called "The Difference Between Pepsi and Coke." Pick a similarly everyday pair—butter and margarine, perhaps, or hot dogs and hamburgers.

Write a poem about the pair.

# Away from Me

Denise Levertov divides her poem "Losing Track" into six **tercets** (three-line stanzas), in which the first and last lines range from four to seven words, while the middle lines have only three (in one case, four) words. An excerpt:

*Long after you have swung back*
*away from me*
*I think you are still with me . . .*

**Write a poem that follows Levertov's tercet structure.**

# Part of the Landscape

If you could be any part of the landscape—a body of water, say, or a mountain, or a tree—what part would you be? Why? What would you see? Would humans interact with you? If so, how?

Write a poem in which you address some of these questions.

# Pale Gold, Yellow Roses

An excerpt from "Gold" by Donald Hall:

*Pale gold of the walls, gold*
*of the centers of daisies, yellow roses*
*pressing from a clear bowl.*

In this poem, Hall describes several different gold things around his house. Pick a color, then write a poem about several different objects of that color.

# My Odd Habit

Write a poem about something you've never told anyone.

It doesn't have to be a huge secret—you could write about a funny habit (like counting the streetlights as you drive down your block) or a weird routine (like always putting your clothes on in a certain order).

# A Confusing World

When you're little, the world is confusing. You might think that your parents whisper at night because they're plotting something sinister, when really they're just trying not to wake you up; you might believe that tiny actors live inside the television and act in all the shows and commercials; or you might worry that you'll be required to read on the first day of school.

**What did you believe as a child that seems completely absurd now? Write about one of these beliefs in a poem.**

# Form and Meaning

It is sometimes said that music is the purest art form, because it combines form and meaning seamlessly. Poetry might be called the form of writing that is closest to music, because the sounds of the words in a poem are just as important as the meaning of those words.

Write a poem in which you focus on the sound of the words—the song of the language—rather than on what the words mean. Consider whether the words are hard or soft, long or short, loud or quiet. Don't worry about grammar or about making perfect sense.

# The Poem Arrives

In "The Poem," Daniel Hoffman imagines his poem making a long, hard journey to completion. The poem finally arrives, "As a sole survivor returns / From the steep pass."

What kind of stages do your poems pass through as you create them? Come up with some concrete images to describe the journey of your poems.

# The Color of a Smell

**Synesthesia** is the evocation of one sense impression through the stimulation of another sense. It is difficult to explain synesthesia, but you've probably experienced it yourself. If you've ever smelled something that made you think of a color, or heard a song that made you recall a certain smell, then you know what synesthesia is.

Write a poem about a synesthetic experience.

# Recent History

In the poem "Blue Streak," by Heather McHugh, the speaker suggests that recent history is characterized by machines and self-involvement, a time when "Kisses came / in twisted foil" and we "invented the pacemaker / in case we fell in love."

Write a poem about your own view of recent history. If you're having trouble getting started, try using "This is history as I see it:" as your first line.

# Talking to Poets

A famous poem by e. e. cummings ends with the line "nobody, not even the rain, has such small hands." In this line, cummings imagines that the rain has a human characteristic: hands. Do you ever think of natural causes or inanimate objects as having human characteristics? For instance, some people talk to plants because they believe the plants can "hear" them.

Write a poem in which you **personify**—or give human characteristics—to an inanimate object.

# Tricky Questions

In "Enigmas," Pablo Neruda describes a series of fantastical, complicated questions and answers. An excerpt:

*You question me about the wicked tusk of the narwhal, and I reply by describing how the sea unicorn with the harpoon in it dies.*

Write a poem in which you ask tricky questions and provide beautiful, complicated answers.

# Morning Freewrite

Write for five minutes about *morning*—whatever that word evokes for you. Try writing continuously, without stopping, for the whole five minutes. It doesn't matter if you write things that seem irrelevant or sound stupid to you; **freewriting** is about letting your thoughts flow without editing them. After the five minutes, go back through what you've written, and pick out a few details that appeal to you.

Using these details, craft a poem of ten lines or less.

# The Fruit of That Forbidden Tree

*Of Man's first disobedience, and the fruit*
*Of that forbidden tree whose mortal taste*
*Brought death into the world and all our woe,*
*With loss of Eden, till one greater Man*
*Restore us and regain the blissful seat . . .*

In the first line and its transition into the second line of the epic poem *Paradise Lost*, Milton makes brilliant use of the literary device called **enjambment**, in which the placement of a word at the end of a line can highlight the importance of that word. By placing the word *fruit* at the end of the first line, Milton draws our attention to its different meanings. Fruit can be what Adam and Eve ate before they were expelled from Eden, or it can be what happened when they ate it (as in the phrase "the fruit of your labors").

Another kind of enjambment is when the line break emphasizes the meaning of a phrase, such as in these lines: "the water / overflows the banks." The water being described actually flows, in a poetic sense, into the next line. Write a poem in which you use a few lines of enjambment.

# Mad Poems

Taking Mad Libs® as a model, write a poem using a few blanks with specified parts of speech underneath. (For example, one line might read, "The sound of __________ during the long, still night.")

[-ing verb]

Then ask a classmate to fill in the blanks—but, as in Mad Libs®, just give her a list of the parts of speech you need filled in. Don't let her see the poem. Insert the words in the poem, and see what you end up with.

# In the Voice

Think of a person you know really well, such as a family member or your best friend. Then write a poem in the voice of that person, trying to capture his or her attitude, habits of speech, and personality.

# Dweeby Philip

In "My Night with Philip Larkin," by Rachel Loden, the speaker imagines spending some time with the poet Philip Larkin. An excerpt:

*Rendezvous with dweeby Philip in the shower . . .*
*I can hear him grumbling through the falling water.*

Write your own imagined rendezvous with someone you admire or would just like to meet.

# Two Lenses

Think of something you've changed your opinion about over the years. For example, maybe you loved playing in the snow when you were little, but now you'd rather stay inside than get cold. Or maybe you used to think the news was boring, but now you find it interesting.

Write two stanzas in which you describe the same thing through two different lenses—one from when you were a child and one from your point of view now.

# One of Those Mornings

Write a poem that begins "It was one of those mornings. . . ." Rather than writing about a personal experience, try making up something that hasn't actually happened to you.

# I Hate, I Love

*I hate and I love. Why should I do this, perhaps you may ask?*
*I do not know, but I feel it happening, and I am troubled.*

In this short poem by Catullus, the speaker feels two contradictory emotions—hate and love—simultaneously.

Make up a story in which something causes the main character to hate and love at the same time. Use Catullus's poem as the last two lines of your story.

# Ourselves Are Lonesome Creatures

In William Meredith's "The Open Sea," the speaker suggests that humans ascribe emotions to natural forces that don't actually have emotions. The speaker says that while we call the sea "lonely," what we should really say is "Ourselves are lonesome creatures whom the sea / Gives neither yes nor no for company." (In poetry, the idea that things have emotions is often called the **pathetic fallacy**.)

Pick a natural force to which people often attach emotions. In your poem, show how the emotion really belongs to the humans, not to the natural force.

# I Had the Weirdest Dream

It's often boring to hear about other people's dreams, but it's endlessly fascinating to talk about your own. Pick a dream that you remember vividly enough to write about, and compose a poem that tells the story of the dream.

# "On First Looking into Chapman's Homer"

*Much have I travell'd in the realms of gold,*
*And many goodly states and kingdoms seen;*
*Round many western islands have I been*
*Which bards in fealty to Apollo hold.*
*Oft of one wide expanse had I been told*
*That deep-brow'd Homer ruled as his demesne;*
*Yet did I never breathe its pure serene*
*Till I heard Chapman speak out loud and bold:*
*Then felt I like some watcher of the skies*
*When a new planet swims into his ken;*
*Or like stout Cortez when with eagle eyes*
*He star'd at the Pacific—and all his men*
*Look'd at each other with a wild surmise—*
*Silent, upon a peak in Darien.*

In this well-known sonnet, John Keats describes reading Chapman's translation of Homer, an ancient Greek poet. Keats is so moved by the beauty of Chapman's language that he compares his reading of the translation to a sky watcher discovering a new planet.

Think of something that touched you in this way. Title your poem "On First Looking into . . . ," followed by the name of whatever it is that moved you.

# Farewell to You

Think of a time you had to say goodbye to someone important to you. Then write a farewell poem to that person. Include as many concrete details as possible, such as where the person was going, why he or she was leaving, and when you might see him or her again.

# "Love Without Hope"

*Love without hope, as when the young bird-catcher*
*Swept off his tall hat to the Squire's own daughter,*
*So let the imprisoned larks escape and fly*
*Singing about her head, as she rode by.*

Short poems like this one by Robert Graves may look easy to write, but it is actually very difficult to get a whole poem's worth of ideas into four lines. To succeed, you need to condense your language, making each word important.

Try writing a four-line poem. Be as precise and concise as possible. You can start from scratch or return to another longer poem you've written and try to condense it into four lines. Don't worry if it takes a long time to write: short poems often take longer to write than long poems.

# Dinner Delight

Write a poem in which you describe your favorite meal—but without mentioning anything about how it tastes or what it looks like. Instead, write about what the meal means to you, what you associate with it, where you usually eat it, or what memories it brings back for you.

# Sorrowful Noise

In Ezra Pound's "The River-Merchant's Wife," the speaker shows her sadness at her lover's departure by saying, "And you have been gone five months. / The monkeys make sorrowful noise overhead." Although the speaker doesn't state "I am sad," we know she is sad because of the way she describes the noise of the monkeys.

Write a poem in which you convey emotion not by naming it, but by ascribing to it a sound or sight.

# BBC Accent

In "Unrelated Incidents," Tom Leonard writes phonetically to capture a certain British accent. For example, he writes "widny wahnt" to show how his speaker would say "would not want." The speaker of the poem says that no one would want to hear the truth spoken by him; people only want to hear the truth spoken by someone with a "BBC" accent (that is, an upper-class British accent).

Try writing a poem phonetically to capture your own accent. Spell the words as wackily as Leonard did, if you need to, in order to make the voice come across.

# Photo Poem

Think of a photograph taken of you. Try to remember the details of the photo—what you are wearing, who you are with, what objects are around you. Then write a poem about the photo.

# A House's History

In his poem "Directive," Robert Frost ruminates on a "house that is no more a house" in a "town that is no more a town." Imagine your house or your town the way it was decades ago. Who lived there, if anyone? What was the land like? Were there stores, or houses, or even roads? Write a poem about it.

# I Will Not Mention

In "Song," by Esther Mathews, the speaker spends the whole poem talking about what she "can't be talkin'" about:

*I can't be talkin' of love, dear,*
*I can't be talkin' of love.*
*If there be one thing I can't talk of*
*That one thing do be love.*

In poetry, this is called **preterition**—a method in which you say "I will not mention . . . " in order to draw attention to exactly the thing you're claiming you don't want to mention. Write a poem in which you use preterition.

# Still Life

A bowl of fruit probably doesn't strike you as very special, yet for centuries great artists have created beautiful, evocative paintings of what are called **still lifes**. Try writing a still life poem.

Pick any object or set of objects and study it or them for a few minutes, just as a painter would. Then write a short, sustained poem that does nothing more than describe what you are looking at.

# "My Heart Leaps Up"

*My heart leaps up when I behold*
*A rainbow in the sky:*
*So was it when my life began;*
*So is it now I am a man:*
*So be it when I shall grow old,*
*Or let me die!*
*The child is father of the man;*
*And I could wish my days to be*
*Bound each to each by natural piety.*

The singsong nature of this poem by William Wordsworth might immediately catch your attention. As an exercise, count out the syllables of each line and mark the accents of the words (i.e., "My *heart* leaps *up* when *I* be*hold* . . ."). Then try writing a poem that copies Wordsworth's singsong meter.

# Familiar Path

Think of a route you take, either daily or several times a year. Maybe it's the route you take to school, to your aunt's house, or to your favorite restaurant.

Imagine something you always see on this trip—a certain billboard, maybe, or a strangely shaped tree—and write a poem about it.

# My Phobia

Is there anything you fear irrationally, such as heights or crowds? Why do you think you are afraid of this thing? Write a poem about your fear.

# Certain Details Are Already Hazy

An excerpt from John Ashbery's "For John Clare":

*You are standing looking at that building and you cannot take it all in, certain details are already hazy and the mind boggles. What will it all be like in five years' time when you try to remember? Will there have been boards in between the grass part and the edge of the street? As long as that couple is stopping to look in that window over there we cannot go.*

This strange and elusive piece is called a **prose poem**. It looks like a regular paragraph, but it has the qualities of a poem.

Write your own prose poem. Don't worry too much about making sense. Instead, focus on the sound of the words and on images. If you need a place to start, feel free to use one of Ashbery's sentences as your first line.

# Family Voices

Write a poem in which each stanza is in the voice of a different member of your family. This will give your poem lots of **perspectives**, or points of view, as opposed to the one sustained perspective you might use in many of your other poems.

# A Chilly Window

In the poem "I Belong There," by Mahmoud Darwish, the speaker talks about his home:

*I belong there. I have many memories. I was born as everyone is born.*
*I have a mother, a house with many windows, brothers, friends, and a prison cell with a chilly window!*

Think about how you feel about your home, what you have learned from living there, and what images you associate with it. Then write a poem that ends with the word *home*.

# You're So Vain

Write a poem about yourself—from the point of view of someone who doesn't like you. How would this person describe you?

# I Was the West

In his poem "Vermont," Dan Chaisson writes about Vermont from the state's perspective. An excerpt:

*I was the west*
*once. I was paradise.*

*My beauty ruined me: the old*
*excuse.*

Write a poem about your state. If you want to, follow Chiasson's example, and make the state the speaker of your poem.

# The ________est Month

T. S. Eliot's famous poem *The Waste Land* begins:

*April is the cruellest month, breeding*
*Lilacs out of the dead land, mixing*
*Memory and desire, stirring*
*Dull roots with spring rain.*

Write a poem that begins in a similar way. Use any month you want and any superlative adjective that fits. For example, you might begin your poem with the line, "June is the softest month."

# Tiger, Ostrich, Mouse

What animal do you most resemble? Write a poem from the point of view of that animal.

# "When I Have Fears That I May Cease to Be"

*When I have fears that I may cease to be*
*Before my pen has glean'd my teeming brain*
*Before high-piled books, in charactery*
*Hold like rich garners the full ripen'd grain.*
*When I behold, upon the night's starr'd face*
*Huge cloudy symbols of a high romance*
*And think that I may never live to track*
*Their shadows, with the magic hand of chance*
*And when I feel, fair creature of an hour*
*That I shall never look upon thee more,*
*Never have relish in the faery power*
*Of unreflecting love; —then on the shore*
*Of the wide world I stand alone, and think*
*Till love and fame to nothingness do sink.*

In this poem by John Keats, the speaker thinks of the things that matter most to him.

Think about a few aspects of your life that you cherish and would hate to leave behind. Write a poem about these aspects.

# Unlocking the Block

If you're ever suffering from writer's block, looking at the newspaper can be a good way of giving yourself some ideas.

Think of a news story you read or heard about recently, and write a poem based on it.

# Sad, Send, Sold

In the poem "I Know a Man," by Robert Creeley, certain words are abbreviated to just two letters. Still, it's easy to figure out what the abbreviations stand for. For example, in the following lines you know *sd* means "said" in this context, even though on its own it could mean a lot of other things—"sad," "send," "sold," etc.

*As I sd to my*
*friend, because I am*
*always talking,-- John, I*

*sd . . .*

Write a poem in which you abbreviate a few words. Make sure a reader could look at the abbreviations and know exactly what they mean.

# There Are Other Fish in the Sea

List a few clichés you've heard over and over again ("Every cloud has a silver lining," "Everything happens for a reason," etc.). Pick one that interests you, and use it as the first or last line of a poem.

# If I Love You at 100 Miles per Hour

In a short story called "Problems" by John Updike, the narrator thinks about his life in terms of algebra and geometry.

Try writing a poem that resembles the question part of a word problem ("If Allan leaves his house at four o'clock and travels at sixty miles per hour . . . "). The word problem can involve problems in a friendship, an important decision, or a mystery. Don't answer your own problem; leave the "calculations" up to the reader.

# I Have Wasted My Life

An excerpt from "Lying in a Hammock at William Duffy's Farm in Pine Island, Minnesota" by James Wright:

*I lean back, as the evening darkens and comes on.*
*A chicken hawk floats over, looking for home.*
*I have wasted my life.*

Wright's poem alters some of the language from Rainer Maria Rilke's "Archaic Torso of Apollo" (which is excerpted in this book on page 16). That poem ends with the line "You must change your life"; this one ends with the line "I have wasted my life."

Write a poem that ends with a surprising line, as Wright's does.

# I Stopped Breathing

An excerpt from Frank O'Hara's poem "The Day Lady Died":

*and I am sweating a lot by now and thinking of*
*leaning on the john door in the 5 SPOT*
*while she whispered a song along the keyboard*
*to Mal Waldron and everyone and I stopped breathing*

O'Hara uses a **stream-of-consciousness** technique in this poem, noting passing images and feelings without bothering with grammar. This technique makes the reader understand the urgency and confusion the speaker feels when he learns of Billie Holiday's death.

Think of a shocking moment in your life and write a poem about it, capturing the feelings you experienced by using stream-of-consciousness techniques.

# Alien View

Think of something you see every day. Now imagine that you're an alien from another planet and have never seen this thing before in your life. Write a poem in which you describe this thing from an alien's point of view.

# The Sound of the Surf

An excerpt from "Corsons Inlet" by A. R. Ammons:

*[I] turned right along*
*the surf*
*rounded a naked headland*
*and returned*

*along the inlet shore . . .*

In this poem, language and sound affect where each line starts. This is unusual; as you've probably noticed, most lines of poetry start on the extreme left side of the page.

Write a poem in which you let rhythm and the meaning of the words dictate where the lines start.

# Pencil, Paper, Pen

Pick up a nearby object—your backpack, a pen—close your eyes, and feel the object with your hands. Write a poem describing the object only in terms of how it feels. Be careful not to include any visual references.

# A Narrow Brush

In the poem "Cash Flow," by Ellen Kaufman, the speaker describes a mundane occurrence: fearing that you've lost your wallet and then finding it a second later:

*No wallet! Blood rushes from your face.*
*You find it though—it's in a different pocket.*
*A narrow brush. These are the precious moments.*

Write a poem about something similarly mundane, like waking up and not knowing what day of the week it is or picking up your foot to continue walking up the staircase and finding you're already at the top.

# Ode to *Splendiferous*

What's your all-time favorite word? Title your poem with this word, and then write a poem about this word as if you're writing an ode to a person.

# The Flap of Pages

In "Reading Myself to Sleep," by Billy Collins, the speaker describes reading at night. An excerpt:

*and the only movement in the night is the slight*
*swirl of curtains, the easy lift and fall of my breathing,*
*and the flap of pages as they turn in the wind of my hand.*

In his poems, Billy Collins often writes about an activity as if he is doing it at that moment.

Try to do the same in a poem of your own.

# Woken from a Dream

Have you ever woken up in the morning and not known where you were, wondered if the dream you just had was real, or thought that maybe your waking life was itself a dream? It is often in these moments of semiconsciousness that the most interesting things happen in our brains.

Think back to one of these moments and try to express it in a poem.

# O World

One of Edna St. Vincent Millay's poems begins, "O world, I cannot hold thee close enough!" Have you ever felt so happy about something or seen something so beautiful that you almost felt overwhelmed by it?

Write a poem that begins or ends with this line of Millay's.

# Miniature Life

In "The Paperweight," by Gjertrud Schnackenberg, the speaker describes looking at a paperweight and observing the small scene inside, where a miniature wife waits on a miniature husband. An excerpt:

*. . . she serves him tea*
*Once and forever, dressed from head to foot*
*As she is always dressed.*

Pick an object that holds some metaphorical meaning for you, and write a poem about it.

# Uncertainties, Mysteries, Doubts

John Keats, the famous poet, is also known for coining the phrase "negative capability." Here is an excerpt from a letter in which he vaguely defines the term:

*Several things dove-tailed in my mind, & at once it struck me, what quality went to form a Man of Achievement, especially in Literature . . . I mean Negative Capability, that is when man is capable of being in uncertainties, Mysteries, doubts, without any irritable reaching after fact & reason.*

Write a short poem about "uncertainties, Mysteries, doubts." Don't try to resolve the uncertainties or even to make sense.

# To Have or Nothing

An excerpt from "Poetry Is a Destructive Force" by Wallace Stevens:

*That's what misery is,*
*Nothing to have at heart.*
*It is to have or nothing.*

In this poem, Stevens offers an abstract vision of poetry. What is poetry to you? Write a poem about it.

# I Am a Russian Tailor

Write a poem about yourself that is filled with lies. Try to make up creative, dramatic lies, rather than saying such things as "I have two cats" or "I love chocolate pudding."

# Lolloping, Lolloping

The poem "Hunting Song," by Donald Finkel, is full of word repetition and rhythm. An excerpt:

*The fox he came lolloping, lolloping,*
*Lolloping. His eyes were bright,*
*His ears were high.*

Write a poem in which you use repetition and rhythm, as Finkel does.

# I Hate Everything About You

Think of someone you can't stand. Then write a humorous love poem about this person.

# Solitary Spot

When you were young, you probably went to a certain place when you wanted to be alone.

Describe that place in a poem, and explain why it was a good spot for solitude.

# Sermons in Stones

A passage from William Shakespeare's play *As You Like It*:

*Sweet are the uses of adversity*
*Which, like the toad, ugly and venomous,*
*Wears yet a precious jewel in his head.*
*And this our life exempt from public haunt,*
*Finds tongues in trees, books in running brooks,*
*Sermons in stones, and good in everything.*

In this speech, Duke Senior describes the Forest of Arden, where he lives in a sort of paradise. Notice how Shakespeare uses **alliteration** (the repetition of consonant sounds) in the last few lines of this passage: "tongues in trees," "books in running brooks," "sermons in stones."

Try using alliteration to describe your Forest of Arden, your place away from reality.

# Bug's-Eye View

Write a poem from the point of view of a bug. How does it spend its day? Where does it live, what does it eat, what does it think about, what does it fear, how does the everyday world look to it?

# Childhood Games

In the voice of your younger self, write a poem about your favorite childhood game. Be as realistic as you can in depicting the way you thought and spoke at that age.

# Imagined Wedding

Write a poem in which you imagine your grandparents' wedding. Where did it take place? Was it a fancy wedding with lots of people or a civil ceremony? Did it take place in a small dusty town? Did anyone try to stop the wedding? What were people wearing? What did they eat at the reception? What was the cake like? Don't feel that you have to answer all of these questions; just use them for inspiration.

# The Sill of the World

In the poem "The Writer," Richard Wilbur describes the plight of a trapped starling that eventually escapes:

*It lifted off from a chair-back,*
*Beating a smooth course for the right window*
*And clearing the sill of the world.*

Wilbur uses **exaggeration** in this poem. When the starling escapes from the house, for example, Wilbur describes him as "clearing the sill of the world"; in reality, of course, the starling is just flying out of the window.

Try using this kind of exaggeration in a poem. Use an image that will make a simple action seem more dramatic.

# Rain on Your Parade

Think of a day when the weather clashed completely with what happened. Perhaps it was dreary and rainy on a day you heard fantastic news, or maybe the sun shone beautifully and insistently on the day your dog died.

Narrate this experience in a poem.

# The Shape of a Swan

The French poet Guillaume Apollinaire was known for his surrealist poems. Many of his poems were in the shape of the thing he was describing, a form known as **concrete**, or **visual**, poetry. For example, a poem about a swan would actually be written in the shape of a swan.

Think of a material or living thing you want to write about, and then shape the language of your poem according to the shape of the object.

# "We Are Seven"

*"The first that died was sister Jane;*
*In bed she moaning lay,*
*Till God released her of her pain;*
*And then she went away.*

*"So in the church-yard she was laid;*
*And, when the grass was dry,*
*Together round her grave we played,*
*My brother John and I.*

*"And when the ground was white with snow,*
*And I could run and slide,*
*My brother John was forced to go,*
*And he lies by her side."*

*"How many are you, then," said I,*
*"If they two are in heaven?"*
*Quick was the little Maid's reply,*
*"O Master! we are seven."*

*"But they are dead; those two are dead!*
*Their spirits are in heaven!"*
*'Twas throwing words away; for still*
*The little Maid would have her will,*
*And said, "Nay, we are seven!"*

The child speaks almost cheerfully about her two dead siblings in this excerpt from William Wordsworth's poem, insisting that she has seven siblings, even though only five are living. Do you remember how you thought about death when you were a young child? Did it confuse you when adults explained that death lasts forever? Write a poem about a child's conception of death. You can use a story, as Wordsworth does, or you can write from a child's perspective.

# A Single Letter

In "Late September," Charles Simic uses slightly eerie images, such as this one:

*The mail truck goes down the coast*
*Carrying a single letter.*

Write a poem that features bizarre, dark details.

# The Story of a Scare

Has there ever been a scare in your town or city, or in a nearby town or city? A fire, a series of burglaries, the death of a young person?

Think of one of these scares, and narrate its story in a poem.

# Ring, Slab, Sound, Globe, Tassel, Something

From one of the first pages of Virginia Woolf's novel *The Waves*:

*"I see a ring," said Bernard, "hanging above me. It quivers and hangs in a loop of light."*
*"I see a slab of pale yellow," said Susan, "spreading away until it meets a purple stripe."*
*"I hear a sound," said Rhoda, "cheep, chirp; cheep chirp; going up and down."*
*"I see a globe," said Neville, "hanging down in a drop against the enormous flanks of some hill."*
*"I see a crimson tassel," said Jinny, "twisted with gold threads."*
*"I hear something stamping," said Louis. "A great beast's foot is chained. It stamps, and stamps, and stamps."*

Woolf writes this entire novel through the dialogue and inner monologues of these six characters. In this part of the novel, each character is describing a sunrise.

Pick a natural phenomenon like this, and write some lines of dialogue, using Woolf's poetic prose as your model, from several different points of view.

# As a Toaster

Write a poem titled "Self-Portrait as . . . . " Pick anything you identify with—an object, an animal, even a street in your town—and describe how whatever you've chosen relates to your own personality. If you picked the color blue, for example, portray yourself as an embodiment of this color.

# When You Were Very Small

Try to recall your earliest memory. Who was there at the time? Where were you, and what were you doing?

Construct a poem about this memory.

# April Showers, May Flowers

Louise Glück once said, “Everyone should write a spring poem.” Write one!

# Hurtling Toward the Cereal, Spoon at the Ready

Write a dramatic account of your morning routine. Use as many grand statements and big words as possible.

# "The River Merchant's Wife"

*At fourteen I married My Lord you.*
*I never laughed, being bashful.*
*Lowering my head, I looked at the wall.*
*Called to, a thousand times, I never looked back.*

*At fifteen I stopped scowling,*
*I desired my dust to be mingled with yours*
*Forever and forever and forever.*
*Why should I climb the lookout?*

*At sixteen you departed,*
*You went into far Ku-to-en, by the river of swirling eddies,*
*And you have been gone five months.*
*The monkeys make sorrowful noise overhead.*
*You dragged your feet when you went out.*
*By the gate now, the moss is grown, the different mosses,*
*Too deep to clear them away!*
*The leaves fall early this autumn, in wind.*
*The paired butterflies are already yellow with August*
*Over the grass in the West garden;*
*They hurt me. I grow older.*
*If you are coming down through the narrows of the river Kiang,*
*Please let me know beforehand,*
*And I will come out to meet you*
*As far as Cho-fo-Sa.*

Using this excerpt from Li Po's poem (translated by Ezra Pound) as a model, write a poem in the form of a letter to an imagined spouse who has gone far away.

# Totally Different—Kind Of

Write a two-stanza poem in which you contrast yourself with another person. In the first stanza, write as if the other person has absolutely nothing in common with you. In the second stanza, admit that you are similar in some ways.

# Baking Bread, Clean Sheets

Write a poem describing a smell from childhood that overwhelms you with nostalgia when you smell it now.

# Breakfast Guest

If you could invite anyone over for breakfast, who would it be? What would you serve this person to eat? What would the conversation be about?

Write a poem that answers these questions.

# Other Times We Don't

The first line from Wislawa Szymborska's "A Few Words on the Soul":

*We have a soul at times.*

What do you think this statement means? Do you agree or disagree with it? Write a poem that responds to this line in some way; you can even use the line as part of your poem if you want.

# Dear Me

Write a poem-letter from your childhood self to your self now. In the poem, give yourself advice, tell yourself what mistakes to avoid, or encourage yourself.

# Dear Me II

Write a poem-letter from your self now to your self in ten years. In the poem, explain what you hope you're doing or talk about your predictions for the future.

# Treasured Room

Write about a room in the house where you were born or spent your early childhood years. What did you cherish in that room? What are the specific objects you remember being in that room?

# Immense Event

In ten lines or less, describe a huge event, such as a war or a lifetime. You can make the poem funny if you want.

# Journey of the Mind

Write a poem about a journey you'd like to take. Where would you go? Whom would you want to travel with? What sorts of things would you pack? Don't feel that you have to answer all of these questions; just use them for inspiration.

# "Leda and the Swan"

*A sudden blow: the great wings beating still*
*Above the staggering girl, her thighs caressed*
*By the dark webs, her nape caught in his bill,*
*He holds her helpless breast upon his breast.*

*How can those terrified vague fingers push*
*The feathered glory from her loosening thighs?*
*And how can body, laid in that white rush,*
*But feel the strange heart beating where it lies?*

*A shudder in the loins engenders there*
*The broken wall, the burning roof and tower*
*And Agamemnon dead.*
*Being so caught up,*
*So mastered by the brute blood of the air,*
*Did she put on his knowledge with his power*
*Before the indifferent beak could let her drop?*

In this poem, W. B. Yeats considers the myth of Leda and the swan, in which Jupiter transforms himself into a swan and flies down to earth to make love to a mortal woman. Several poets besides Yeats have written about this myth, including Rainer Maria Rilke.

Choose a myth that interests you and write a poem in which you retell it.

# Hunting for the Bizarre

Freewrite for five minutes on whatever topic comes to mind. When five minutes have passed, go back through what you've written, and pick out the most bizarre sentence or phrase. Then write a poem that uses this sentence or phrase as its first line.

# Another Life

Write a poem from the point of view of a homeless person.

# Talking of Michelangelo

*In the room the women come and go*
*Talking of Michelangelo*

These two excerpted lines are a refrain that T. S. Eliot uses throughout "The Love Song of J. Alfred Prufrock" between different stanzas. The image of the women talking about Michelangelo has nothing to do with the rest of the poem, and the poet never makes any connection between this refrain and what's going on in the longer stanzas.

Think of a two-line observation like this one, and make it your refrain. Then write a three-stanza poem in which you use the refrain twice. See if you can make the refrain completely disconnected from the rest of the poem.

# Future Family

Write a poem in which you describe your future family, but don't use the future tense. Instead, write as if your future family already exists. How many kids are in your family? Where do you live? Do you get along? Don't feel that you have to answer all of these questions; just use them for inspiration.

# Lost City

Write about a place you've studied in your history or social studies class—a place that no longer exists. In your poem, try to make this place come to life by using clear visual details.

# Metaphor Mishaps

All writers use **figurative language** to describe things that are otherwise difficult to describe. But **metaphors** and **similes** can be dangerous when misused, as you'll see from these examples:

*Her face was a perfect oval, like a circle that had its two other sides gently compressed by a Thigh Master.*

*His thoughts tumbled in his head, making and breaking alliances like underpants in a dryer without Cling Free™.*

*The little boat gently drifted across the pond exactly the way a bowling ball wouldn't.*

Come up with three humorous metaphors of your own.

# Detached Intensity

Think of an event from the past that affected you intensely—an emotional experience from your childhood, perhaps, or your first crush, or the way you felt when you first read your favorite book.

Write about this perspective from an objective point of view, as if you're an outside observer. To help keep your poem detached, write in the **third person** (refer to yourself as "he" or "she," instead of using "I").

# I'm So Sorry

Write an apology to someone in the form of a poem.

# "Ozymandius of Egypt"

*I met a traveller from an antique land*
*Who said:—Two vast and trunkless legs of stone*
*Stand in the desert. Near them on the sand,*
*Half sunk, a shatter'd visage lies, whose frown*
*And wrinkled lip and sneer of cold command*
*Tell that its sculptor well those passions read*
*Which yet survive, stamp'd on these lifeless things,*
*The hand that mock'd them and the heart that fed.*
*And on the pedestal these words appear:*
*"My name is Ozymandias, king of kings:*
*Look on my works, ye mighty, and despair!"*
*Nothing beside remains: round the decay*
*Of that colossal wreck, boundless and bare,*
*The lone and level sands stretch far away.*

In this poem by Percy Bysshe Shelley, the speaker talks about King Ozymandias and his downfall. Only a broken statue of the once-powerful king now remains. Think of something you take for granted, something you assume will last forever.

Write a poem in which you imagine what it would be like if this thing was taken away.

# My Life So Far

In a poem, tell the story of your life so far. Your poem can be funny, dramatic, or serious.

# About Poetry

Write a poem about your approach to poetry. What is difficult about it for you? What do you like about it? What, to you, are the exciting aspects of poetry? What aspects do you dislike? Don't feel that you have to answer all of these questions; just use them as inspiration.

# Talking Alone

Write a dramatic monologue of someone talking to himself or herself. This person could be you, someone you've overheard, or someone you make up. Try to capture the way people talk when they think no one is listening.

# A Talking Dog

In Stephen Dobyns's poem "How to Like It," the speaker's dog suggests making a giant sandwich, and the speaker takes his suggestion:

*. . . and that's where the man's*
*wife finds him, staring into the refrigerator*
*as if into the place where the answers are kept . . .*

In this poem, Dobyns gets across some very serious and profound ideas with the fantastical conceit of a talking dog.

Write a poem in which you present something totally impossible as unremarkable and common.

# King Kong Questions

In her poem "Seventeen Questions about King Kong," Jane Cooper writes a list of questions on one topic. She never answers any of them. An excerpt:

*But why is New York, the technological marvel, so distrusted, when technologically the film was unsurpassed for its time?*

*Must the anthropologist always dream animal dreams? Must we?*

Try writing a similarly abstract poem that is made up of one question after another.

# Poem™

Write a poem that uses as many brand names as you can think of. The topic of this poem is entirely up to you.

# Old-Fashioned

What historical era do you think you would have enjoyed living in?

Write a poem from the perspective of someone or something living in that era. Be as clear and detailed as possible so that someone reading your poem might be able to guess what era you're describing.

# I Dreamed a Dream

When you were growing up, did you have a recurring dream or nightmare? Write a poem about this recurring dream. Express the emotions you felt in the dream, and describe how the dream began and ended.

# "George Gray"

*I have studied many times*
*The marble which was chiseled for me—*
*A boat with a furled sail at rest in a harbor.*
*In truth it pictures not my destination*
*But my life.*
*For love was offered me and I shrank from its disillusionment;*
*Sorrow knocked at my door, but I was afraid;*
*Ambition called to me, but I dreaded the chances.*
*Yet all the while I hungered for meaning in my life.*
*And now I know that we must lift the sail*
*And catch the winds of destiny*
*Wherever they drive the boat.*
*To put meaning in one's life may end in madness,*
*But life without meaning is the torture*
*Of restlessness and vague desire—*
*It is a boat longing for the sea and yet afraid.*

This poem is from Edgar Lee Masters's book *Spoon River Anthology,* a collection of fictitious accounts by dead people looking back on their lives from the grave.

Make up a life story for someone, and write a poem in which the person looks back on his or her life after it has ended. Use the **first person** (the pronoun "I"), as "George Gray" does. If you like, you can include something about how the person died.

# I Swear I'll Never . . .

Many kids get angry at certain habits their parents have and swear they'll treat their own kids differently.

Write a poem in list form about things you want to remember when you're a parent. Try to include all the things you think it might be easy to forget as you get older.

# How Do I Love Thee?

Write a love poem to someone you don't like. Working on poems that don't have much to do with your real emotions will help your poetry become more disciplined and less sentimental.

# There Is No Frigate Like a Book

*There is no Frigate* like a Book* — *ship
*To take us Lands away*
*Nor any coursers* like a Page* — *horses or dogs
*Of prancing Poetry—*
*This Traverse* may the poorest take* — *path
*Without oppress* of Toll*—* — *burden, tax
*How frugal* is the Chariot* — *humble, poor
*That bears* the Human soul.* — *carries or contains

Emily Dickinson's poem compares reading to traveling by using several metaphors—comparisons that don't use the words *like* or *as*. (In Greek, the word *metaphor* literally means "transport," which makes metaphors an appropriate device for this poem.) A series of metaphors like the one in this poem is called an **extended metaphor**. Read the poem again and see how many comparisons between books and journeys you can find. Then come up with an extended metaphor of your own.

Write a poem using a few of those metaphors to convey—to transport—your ideas.

# At the Peak

Have you ever felt like you were on top of the world, literally? Have you ever stood on a cliff, climbed to the top of a mountain, or looked out the window of a skyscraper?

Write a poem about the experience. Include a description of the view.

# Wish Upon a Poem

Write a poem about something you wish would happen tomorrow.

# Haiku for You

**Moss**
*Lacey fuzz atop*
*a sheen of dreggy water*
*nurturing network*

**Sunset**
*Dark insinuates*
*Pallid gleams and popping stars*
*the sun expires.*

**Butterfly**
*A million pigments*
*Flutter on creamy palettes*
*Cavalier beauty*

A **haiku** is a poem that consists of seventeen syllables and three lines. The first line has five syllables, the second has seven, and the third has five.

Write a haiku of your own. But don't feel that you have to stick to a topic from nature, as these traditional haiku do; you can write about anything you like.

# Prayer of a Pariah

In "To the Brooklyn Bridge," Hart Crane writes an ode to the landmark bridge, which he calls "Terrific threshold of the prophet's pledge, / Prayer of pariah, and the lover's cry."

Think of a landmark in your state that defines part of the culture or just defines part of your own life. Then write an ode to this landmark.

# Letter to a Loner

Imagine that someone your age lives on a deserted island and refuses to be rescued. Send this island inhabitant a message in a bottle, in the form of a poem. You can ask this person to come home, talk about your own life, or ask what life on the island is like.

# Whose Leg Is This?

In the chapter "The Man Who Fell out of Bed" from *The Man Who Mistook His Wife for a Hat*, Oliver Sacks writes of a man suffering from a strange neurological problem:

*He had felt fine all day, and fallen asleep towards evening. When he woke up he felt fine too, until he moved in the bed. Then he found, as he put it, "someone's leg" in the bed—a severed human leg, a horrible thing! He was stunned, at first, with amazement and disgust—he had never experienced, never imagined, such an incredible thing. He felt the leg gingerly. It seemed perfectly formed, but "peculiar" and "old."*

*When the patient tried to throw the leg out of the bed, he fell out with it. It turned out that this "other" leg was actually the patient's own leg, which his brain had somehow stopped recognizing.*

Write a poem from the point of view of this man, who sees his leg as grotesque because he cannot recognize it as his own. Try to imagine what it might feel like to have something attached to your boyd that seems terribly unfamiliar, as well as disgusting.

# Portrait in Personality

Write a poem-portrait of a person in your class. Don't describe the physical appearance of this person or the way he or she dresses. Instead, come up with other ways to describe this person. Then switch poems with someone near you, and see if you can guess the subject of each other's poem-portraits.

# Hanging Fire

In "Hanging Fire," Audre Lorde writes about a girl who has many of the fears and worries any teenager has—not fitting in, dying, feeling isolated from her parents, etc. A closer look, however, reveals the added struggle the speaker faces as an African-American girl:

*I am fourteen*
*and my skin has betrayed me*

Write a poem about a time when you felt left out or different. Use the **first-person voice** ("I"), as Lorde does.

# Um, Like, [Pause]

Try writing a poem in dialogue. If you want, find inspiration in a conversation you overheard recently. Try to capture the way people actually talk. Incorporate "ums," "likes," and pauses into your poem.

# On the Outside

Think about a time you felt out of place socially. Do you think you felt uncomfortable because of the way someone was treating you, or was it just because you were self-conscious?

Write a poem about how it felt to be an outsider.

# The Most Beautiful

Write a poem about the most beautiful thing you have ever seen.

# Shadow Seeks Shadow

In "Evening," the poet H. D. writes a clear, fluid, simple description of evening. Her poem ends with these lines:

*shadow seeks shadow,*
*then both leaf*
*and leaf-shadow are lost.*

Write a poem describing anything you want, trying to mimic H. D.'s clear style. Use strong, earthy words, instead of complicated ones. Don't worry about having a "point"; just focus on describing whatever you've chosen.

# You Stare and You Wait

An excerpt from "In Celebration," by Mark Strand:

*so you wait, you stare and you wait, and the dust settles*
*and the miraculous hours of childhood wander in darkness.*

How would you define the "miraculous hours of childhood"? Write a poem about whatever this phrase means to you.

# Sunny Blizzard

Describe your personality by writing a poem about the weather. For example, if you are a moody, unkind person, you might write a poem about green summer skies and loud thunder. Don't feel that you have to write realistically about the weather. If a sunny blizzard best describes your personality, feel free to write about that.

# The Room in the Dark

Write a poem about what your room looks like at night. Do shadows move around the walls? Do car headlights shine into your room? Do you hear certain sounds every night? Don't feel that you have to answer all of these questions in your poem; just use them for inspiration.

# Ideal Reader

In "Selecting a Reader," Ted Kooser imagines the ideal reader of his poems. He envisions her flipping through a book of his poems in the bookstore and then saying, "'For that kind of money, I can get / my raincoat cleaned.' And she will."

Imagine your ideal reader, and write a poem in which you describe this person encountering your poetry.

# Through the Facts

Write a poem in which each line consists of one simple fact, such as "sometimes it rains" or "sadness settles on me in the winter." Try to tell a story through facts alone.

# Palpable and Mute

An excerpt from "Ars Poetica" by Archibald MacLeish:

*A poem should be palpable and mute*
*As a globed fruit,*

*Dumb*
*As old medallions to the thumb,*

*Silent as the sleeve-worn stone*
*Of casement ledges where the moss has grown--*

*A poem should be wordless*
*As the flight of birds.*

Write your own *ars poetica* (from the Latin for "poetic craft"). In your poem, explain what a poem should be.

# The Highest Candle

In his poem "Final Soliloquy of the Interior Paramour," Wallace Stevens posits that the human imagination is the "highest candle," the light that reaches the farthest up into the darkness of what we don't know and can't fathom. To Stevens, the imagination is an amazing thing—the poem exclaims, "How high that highest candle lights the dark."

What "lights the dark" for you? Is it a poem, an object, a place you've known all your life? Describe this person, object, or place in a poem. Include Stevens's line, "How high that highest candle lights the dark."

# Present at the Birth

Write a poem about your own birth. Where were you? How did you come out of your mother's body? Were you reluctant to leave the womb? Who was present at your birth? What did it feel like to enter the world? Don't feel that you have to answer all of these questions; just use them for inspiration.

# All Alone

Have you ever been truly lost? Write a poem about the fear or excitement you felt when you realized you had no idea where you were.

# A Phony Old Construct

In "Excerpt: Index of First Lines," Mary Winters creates a poem that looks like the *S* section of an imaginary index. An excerpt:

*Sanitize my memoirs? I think not,* 392
*Sanity's a phony old construct,* 18

Think of funny or thought-provoking phrases that all start with the same letter, like Winters's, and write an index poem of your own. Be sure to alphabetize your list and add page numbers so that a reader could "find" your ideas.

# From On High

Imagine that you could look out the window of any building in the world. Where would the building be? What would you see as you looked out the window?

Write a poem about the imagined experience.

# Why the Sky Is Blue

Think of something you know nothing about—how a television works, for example, or why mosquito bites itch. Then write a poem in which you explain this phenomenon. Be as fanciful or funny as you want.

# Lost Object

Little kids can feel deep attachments to material things: some cry when their parents sell an old car or protest at the idea of moving to a new house. Write a poem about an object you loved as a child and were forced to give up.

# The Last Fire

In "For the Anniversary of My Death," W. S. Merwin thinks about the date of his death:

*Every year without knowing it I have passed the day*
*When the last fires will wave to me*

In these lines, the speaker thinks of his death as a dead star, as if it has already happened but the "light" of it has not reached him yet.

Think of a scientific phenomenon that interests you—photosynthesis, for example, or the way lightning works, or what glass is made of—and incorporate it into a poem.

# The Strangest Taste

Write a poem about something you like that everyone else hates. You might write about the smell of skunk spray, getting caught in the pouring rain, or the taste of brussels sprouts. Explain why you like this thing. Be as convincing as you can.

# Prompt Yourself

Come up with a poetry prompt of your own. Then switch with one of your classmates, and follow his or her instructions. Share the poems with your class to see what kinds of prompts other people thought up.